I Adore You Until It Hurts

Viv

A Book By:
FOREVER SHININGS

Book Title: I Adore You Until It Hurts

Book Author: Viv

Published By: Forever Shinings

First Edition: 2025

ISBN: 978-93-7406-589-1

She didn't say goodbye.
She just faded out of my life
like it was the easiest thing to do.

So, I wrote this.

Not to make her miss me.
Not to explain myself.
Not to look strong.

I wrote this
because some endings don't happen properly,
and the words stay stuck inside you.

This book is everything

I kept silent about
while pretending I was okay.

This book isn't sweet at all.
It holds things I never said,
feelings I hide well,
and moments I never got closure for.

Read it slowly.
Take breaks if you need to.

If you're still trying to heal,
don't rush through it.

And if a part of you is still waiting
for them to come back—
you might want to stop
before the last page.

obviously for you,

sweety.

NOTE TO THE READERS

See, this book isn't for everyone.
And that's okay,

If you move on easily like you are
idgaf kind of person,
if you don't reread old chats,
if you don't stare at your phone at 2 a.m. hoping a name shows up that never does—-
this book might not be for you.

But if you stayed longer than you should've,
if the person you loved slowly stopped choosing you,
if you went quiet instead of angry,
if you learned to swallow things just to keep someone
-then yeah… this is for you.

I didn't write this to heal you.
I wrote this because I couldn't keep
it inside anymore.

Pretending I was okay hurt more
than bleeding on pages.

Some lines here will feel personal.
That's not accidental.

Some parts will feel uncomfortable.
That's the truth.

Read this slowly.
Put it down when it hurts.

Come back when you're ready.

And if at some point you think,
"fuck… this feels like my story" —-
I'm sorry.

And you're not alone.
Us…

I didn’t know how to begin this
without sounding dramatic.

So I didn’t.
I just started remembering.

You were easy to talk to.
That's how it started.

Not sparks.
Not chaos.

Just comfort that didn't ask questions.
Just silence that didn't feel empty.

I didn't know comfort could leave too.

I don't know why I'm still talking to you like this, but this is how my head works now. It keeps going back to you like you're still listening. Maybe you're not. Maybe you muted everything a long time ago. Still, this is the only way I know how to breathe lately, so I'll say it anyway.

I didn't come into your life trying to be special. I wasn't trying to impress you or play any role. I was just there. Talking. Listening. Trying to make you feel lighter when you said things were heavy. That's it. I didn't know that being available, being honest, being straightforward would slowly turn into something you'd doubt. I didn't know that caring too much would start looking like manipulation in your eyes.

You always say I explain too much. But do you know why I explain? Because I never wanted you to misunderstand me. Because every time you doubted me, it felt like I was losing you a little. So yeah, I talked. I clarified. I repeated myself. I begged sometimes, not because I wanted control, but because I wanted you to see me. I wanted you to know I wasn't hiding anything. There was never a second life, never a backup plan, never another option waiting on the side.

I changed myself in ways I didn't even notice at first. I cut people off. I went quiet where I used to laugh. I stayed awake late even when it was hard, because that was the only time I could talk to you freely. I didn't complain. I didn't count sacrifices. I thought that's what love looks like — adjusting until the other person feels safe. I didn't know I was slowly erasing myself in the process.

You fought a lot. Over small things. Over things that didn't even exist. And every time you said the word "breakup," something inside me collapsed. You said it casually. I heard it like a threat. Like a warning that I could lose everything any second. So, I became softer. Quieter. More apologetic. Even when I didn't know what I had done wrong, I still said sorry, because distance scared me more than losing my self-respect.

I cried in ways I never knew I could. Not loudly. Not dramatically. Just silently, at night, staring at the phone, trying to understand how someone who says "I love you" can also be so cold the next moment. You never held me when I broke down. You said you were upset too. And I believed you, even when I was shaking inside.

I never asked you to stop living your life. I just wanted to feel like I mattered in it. Like my feelings had some weight. But every time I said that, you called it control. Every time I felt jealous, you called it insecurity. Maybe it was. But jealousy doesn't come from nothing. It comes from feeling replaceable. From watching someone else get the softness you stopped giving me.

I trusted you with everything. My thoughts, my fears, my passwords, my vulnerability. I never protected myself from you because I thought love meant transparency. And still, you doubted me. Still, you believed strangers over me. Still, you assumed the worst before asking me once, calmly, what the truth was.

Do you know what hurts the most? Not that you left. But that when I was at my lowest, when I was scared, broken, barely holding myself together — you blamed me. I needed support. I needed reassurance. I needed you to stand beside me. Instead, you made me feel like a problem you wanted to get rid of.

I stayed even then. I stayed because I loved you in a way that didn't know how to leave. I stayed because I thought love means endurance. Because I thought if I just hold on a little longer, you'll see me. You'll understand. You'll stop doubting.

I didn't know some people don't want clarity. They want distance without guilt.

I won't lie — I still think about you. Not because I think you'll come back. But because my mind hasn't learned how to live without you yet. You were my comfort. My focus. The person I imagined a future with. And when that disappeared, everything else felt pointless for a while.

I'm not writing this to accuse you. I'm not writing this to make you feel bad. I'm writing this because I need you to know that what we had was real to me. That I didn't pretend. That I didn't play games. That I didn't love halfway. If that makes me look foolish, I'll accept that. But don't tell me it wasn't genuine.

I loved you deeply. In a way that changed me. In a way that cost me parts of myself. And maybe you didn't feel it the same way. Maybe you never will. But this is my truth. This is how it felt from my side. Raw. Unfiltered. Painful. Real.

I'm learning to let go now. Slowly. Badly. With setbacks. But I'm learning. Not because I stopped loving you, but because I need to start choosing myself the way I kept choosing you.

That's all.
Nothing dramatic.

Just the truth I never got to say without being interrupted.

I'm angry at you. I need to say that first, because pretending I'm not is exhausting. I'm angry because I loved you honestly and you kept doubting me like I was hiding something. I'm angry because every time I tried to explain myself, you called it drama. Like my feelings were noise you wanted to mute, not something you wanted to understand. I'm angry because you made me feel guilty for loving you the way I did.

You don't know what it's like to be constantly questioned by the person you're trying your hardest to protect. To feel like you're standing in court every day, proving your loyalty, your intentions, your heart. I didn't have secrets. I didn't have backups. I didn't have anyone else. And still, you looked at me like I was capable of hurting you on purpose. That fucked me up.

There were nights I wanted to grab your face and ask you to just look at me properly. Not to accuse. Not to assume. Just to see me. To see how tired I was. To see how much effort it took for me to stay calm when you were pushing me away and pulling me back at the same time. That push-pull thing did something ugly to my head. It made me obsessive in ways I never wanted to be.

I hated how much power you had over me. How your mood could ruin my entire day. How one cold reply could make my chest feel tight. I hated checking my phone and feeling relief instead of happiness when you replied. That's not love. That's anxiety dressed up as attachment. And I still stayed.

I wanted you so badly sometimes. Not just emotionally. Physically. The kind of want that makes you forget pride. I wanted to pull you close, kiss you slow, remind you we were real. I wanted to feel you relax against me again, wanted to feel that moment where you stopped fighting everything and just existed with me. Those kisses weren't about desire alone — they were about reassurance. About proving to myself that we still had something worth saving.

But even intimacy started feeling confusing. One moment you were close, soft, needy. The next you were distant, guarded, gone. That inconsistency messed with me. It made me crave you more and resent you at the same time. I hated myself for wanting you when you were hurting me. That contradiction tore me apart quietly.

You used the word "toxic" a lot. Maybe I was becoming that. But you never asked why. You never noticed how scared I was of losing you. How every fight felt like a countdown.

How every silence felt like punishment. I didn't want control. I wanted certainty. I wanted to feel safe loving you.

Sometimes I think you enjoyed having the upper hand. Not intentionally, maybe. But you knew I cared more. You knew I'd stay. You knew I'd explain. And knowing that made it easier for you to pull away without consequences. That hurts to admit, but it's how it felt.

I wasn't perfect. I got jealous. I got insecure. I got emotional. But none of that came from nothing.

It came from watching you slowly detach while expecting me to stay the same. It came from loving someone who kept one foot out the door while I was all in.

I wanted to scream sometimes. Instead, I went quiet. I wanted to leave sometimes. Instead, I begged myself to be patient. I wanted to protect myself. Instead, I chose you. Over and over again. And that choice cost me more than you'll ever know.

I still don't understand how you could say you loved me and still make me feel so alone. That contradiction keeps looping in my head. Maybe you loved me in your way.

Maybe my way was just heavier. But don't tell me I imagined this. Don't tell me I made it all up. What I felt was real. The pain was real. The damage is real.

I don't miss you the way I used to. Now it's mixed with anger. With questions. With things I never got answers to. And maybe that's okay. Maybe this anger is part of letting go. Or maybe it's just the part where I finally stop blaming myself for everything that went wrong.

I loved you. Deeply. Recklessly. In a way that didn't protect me enough. And yeah, that's on me. But don't mistake my love for weakness. It took strength to feel this much and still stay soft.

I don't hate you. That surprised me. After everything, after the anger, after the nights where my chest felt too tight to breathe, I thought hatred would be easier. Cleaner. But it never came. What came instead was this slow, dull understanding that some people don't hurt you because they're cruel — they hurt you because they don't know how to stay once things get real.

I'm tired now. Not sad in the loud way. Just tired in the bones. The kind of tired that comes after you've replayed everything enough times to finally accept there's nothing new left to discover.

No hidden meaning. No secret explanation that'll suddenly make it all make sense. Just two people who loved differently and collided at the wrong time.

I stopped waiting for messages that won't come. Not as an act of strength — just because my body doesn't jump anymore when my phone lights up. That habit faded quietly. And when I noticed, I didn't feel proud. I felt empty. Like something familiar had left without asking permission.

I still think about you sometimes. Mostly at night. Mostly when things slow down. Not because I want your back, but because my mind hasn't fully learned how to exist without the space you occupied. You were woven into my routine, my thoughts, my future plans. Untangling that takes time. I'm not rushing it.

I've stopped asking myself what I could've done differently. That question only leads to self-blame, and I'm done carrying responsibility that wasn't entirely mine. I showed up. I stayed. I tried. That has to count for something, even if it didn't save us.

There are moments I miss the closeness. The way you softened when you trusted me. The way you'd lean in without thinking.

Those memories still hurt a little. But they don't own me anymore. They exist without demanding anything in return.

I'm learning to sit with myself again. Without distraction. Without explaining my feelings to anyone. Just letting things be what they are. Some days feel okay. Some days feel heavy. I'm not labelling either one as progress or failure. They're just days.

I don't need closure from you anymore. I don't need an apology, or a conversation that finally clears things up. I've made peace with the fact that some endings don't arrive neatly. They just... stop. And you have to build your life around the absence.

I still care about you. That truth doesn't disappear just because things ended. But caring doesn't mean chasing anymore. It doesn't mean staying where I'm not chosen. It doesn't mean shrinking myself to fit someone else's comfort. I've learned that lesson the hard way.

Letting go doesn't feel like relief. It feels like loosening a grip that's been clenched for too long. It hurts at first.

Then it feels strange. Then one day, you realize you're holding nothing — and somehow, that's okay.

This isn't me becoming cold. It's me becoming careful. It's me choosing not to bleed for people who don't know how to hold what I give. I'm still soft. Just not reckless anymore.

You were real to me. What we had was real to me. And I'll carry that without turning it into a wound I reopen every night. That's the best goodbye I know how to give.

I'm walking forward now. Slowly. Not because I forgot you — but because I don't want to lose myself again.

That's it.
No dramatic ending.
Just acceptance sitting quietly where hope used to be.

I keep wanting to tell you small things, stupid things, like how my day went or how I saw something that reminded me of you, and then I remember you're not my person anymore. That pause hits harder than the memory itself. I never realized how much space you took in my head until I had to force myself to stop talking to you.

I didn't love you loudly. I loved you in consistency. In showing up. In choosing you even when it was uncomfortable. That's why it hurts now — because you didn't leave something dramatic behind. You left a routine. And routines are harder to kill.

Sometimes I miss you in very physical ways. Like wanting to pull you closer, wanting to feel your weight against me, wanting to kiss you slowly just to remind myself we're real. That craving still shows up randomly and I hate how honest it is.

I used to hold you like I was afraid you'd disappear if I loosened my grip. I didn't know back then that love doesn't disappear because you let go — it disappears when only one person is holding.

You don't know this, but I memorized the way you breathe when you're calm. That's the version of you I still miss — not the distant one, not the confused one — the soft one who trusted me without thinking.

I keep replaying moments where I should’ve spoken up. Not to fight. Just to say, “Hey, this hurts.” But I stayed quiet because I didn’t want to make things heavier. Funny how silence ended up being the heaviest thing.

I loved kissing you in that slow, unplanned way. Not rushed. Not hungry. Just enough to feel connected. Those kisses weren't about desire — they were about reassurance. About saying "we're okay" without words.

There were nights I stayed awake just because you were still awake. I didn't even need to talk. I just liked knowing we existed at the same time. Losing that feels lonelier than being alone.

I changed myself in ways I didn't notice until you were gone. Became quieter. Less expressive. More careful. I don't blame you for that, but I wish you'd noticed what it was costing me.

Sometimes I wonder if you ever felt as safe with me as I felt with you. Not protected — just understood. That's the part I miss the most. Being understood without having to explain.

I still remember how your body relaxed when I held you close. Like you finally stopped carrying the world for a second. I liked being that place for you. I didn't know it would disappear so easily.

I wasn’t asking for perfection. I was asking for effort. For presence. For honesty. And somehow that made me feel like I was asking for too much.

I miss the version of me that believed love was enough. That version was naïve, but genuine. I don't know when I stopped believing, but I know it was while loving you.

There are moments I still want to text you. Not because I think it'll change anything. Just because my instinct still goes to you. Unlearning that is harder than I expected.

I used to imagine holding you from behind, chin resting on your shoulder, no talking, just existing. That image still lives somewhere in me. I don't visit it often. It hurts too much.

You didn't break me. You exhausted me. And that's worse. Broken things want fixing. Exhausted things just want rest.

I hate how easily my body remembers you. The way my hands still crave yours. The way closeness still feels incomplete without you. Logic doesn't help with that.

I never wanted control. I wanted certainty. I wanted to know I wasn't replaceable. I wanted to know I mattered in your life the way you mattered in mine.

I loved you in ways I didn't protect myself from. That's on me. But don't tell me it wasn't real. Real things leave real damage.

If I’m being honest, part of me still hopes you’d read this and finally understand me. Not come back. Just understand. That hope is stupid, but it’s human.

I don't miss the fights. I miss the in-between moments. The way you'd sit close without thinking. The way your hand would find mine automatically. Losing those small, unconscious gestures hurts more than losing the big stuff.

Sometimes I think about how I used to calm you down. Not by fixing anything. Just by being there. I liked knowing I could do that for you. I didn't know that role could be taken away without warning.

There were kisses that felt like comfort, not hunger. Soft ones. Slow ones. The kind that says "stay" without asking. Those are the ones that still mess with me.

I hated how careful I became with my words around you. Like one wrong sentence could push you further away. Love shouldn't feel like walking on glass, but that's how it started to feel.

I don't think you ever realized how much I paid attention to you. The small changes in your tone. The way your energy shifted. I noticed everything and still chose to stay quiet.

I miss holding you when the world felt heavy for you. When you'd finally relax and let yourself be vulnerable. That trust meant everything to me. Losing it feels personal.

There are moments I wish I could rewind to. Not to change anything. Just to sit in them a little longer. To be more present. To know what I was about to lose.

I didn't fall out of love with you. I fell into confusion. And confusion eats you alive slowly. It makes you doubt yourself more than the other person.

I still crave closeness in the way I had it with you. Not just bodies touching. Souls close. Silence comfortable. That kind of intimacy is hard to replace.

You don't know how many times I almost asked you, "Are you still here with me?" I swallowed that question every time because I was scared of the answer.

I loved when you let your guard down around me. When you didn't try to be strong. That version of you felt real. I miss that honesty.

Sometimes I wonder if you noticed how I started pulling back emotionally before you left. That wasn't indifference. That was self-preservation kicking in too late.

There were nights I held you tighter than usual. Not to be possessive. Just because something inside me was afraid of losing you.

I hate how much my body still remembers you. The way my arms expect you to be there. The way closeness feels incomplete now.

I wasn't perfect. I got insecure. I overthought. But none of that came from nowhere. It came from loving someone who felt like they were slipping away.

I miss how natural everything felt before it became complicated. Before love turned into something we had to manage instead of just feel.

There are days I feel fine. And then there are days where I miss you for no clear reason. Those are the hardest ones.

I don't regret loving you the way I did. I regret not protecting myself sooner. That's the part I'm still learning.

I keep reminding myself that wanting you doesn't mean I should go back. Those are two different things, even if they feel similar sometimes.

If I'm honest, part of me still wants you to miss me. Not to come back. Just to feel that what we had mattered as much to you as it did to me.

I started noticing how much control your absence had over me. One unread message could ruin my mood. One cold reply could mess with my entire night. I hated that power, but I didn't know how to take it back without losing you.

There were times I wanted to pull you close and ask you to stay, not with words, just with my body. To kiss you slowly, deeply, until you stopped drifting away. I wanted closeness to fix what talking couldn't.

I don't think you understood how loud my head got when you went quiet. Silence felt like punishment. Like I was being tested without knowing the rules.

I loved the way you fit against me. Not just physically, but emotionally. Like you belonged there without effort. Losing that sense of belonging feels like losing balance.

I hated how I started questioning myself. Wondering if I was too much. Too emotional. Too intense. Loving you made me doubt parts of myself I was once sure about.

There were moments I felt jealous and immediately felt guilty for it. I didn't want to be that person. But jealousy doesn't come from nowhere — it comes from fear.

I still remember the way your lips felt when you kissed me slowly. Those kisses weren't about passion alone. They were about reassurance. About grounding. I miss that kind of touch.

I kept trying to read between your lines, searching for signs that you still cared. That habit exhausted me more than any argument ever did.

I wanted to be the place you came back to when things got heavy. Instead, I became the place you slowly left.

I hated how patient I became. How I learned to wait without complaining. That patience cost me more than you'll ever know.

There were nights I held my phone, not to text you, just to feel close to you somehow. That's when I knew attachment had crossed into something unhealthy.

I miss the way your body softened when you trusted me. When you stopped fighting everything and just existed with me. That trust disappearing hurt deeply.

I don't think you ever saw how much effort it took for me to stay calm when I was scared of losing you. I was fighting myself every day.

I started apologizing for things I didn't fully understand. Not because I was wrong, but because I didn't want distance.

There were times I wanted to mark you as mine in the quietest ways. Holding you longer. Kissing you deeper. Not to claim you — just to feel secure.

I noticed how your energy changed around me. Less warmth. Less curiosity. That shift hurt more than words ever could.

I don’t miss the version of you that pulled away. I miss the version of you that felt present. That distinction matters.

I hated how my happiness started depending on you. That loss of control scared me, but not enough to make me leave.

I wanted you in ways that felt almost desperate at times. Not just emotionally — physically too. Desire became tangled with fear.

Loving you stopped feeling safe before it stopped feeling good. That's when I should've walked away, but I didn't.

I stopped feeling excited to talk to you and started feeling nervous instead. Like every conversation could either save us or ruin us. That pressure slowly killed the joy.

I hated how much I needed reassurance and hated myself more for needing it from you specifically. That dependence made me feel weak in ways I wasn't ready to admit.

There were moments I wanted to shake you and ask what changed. Not angrily. Desperately. Because I could feel you slipping and didn't know how to hold on without hurting us both.

I miss the way you used to look at me when you were fully present. Not distracted. Not guarded. Just there. That look made everything else feel manageable.

I don't think you realized how many times I chose silence over honesty just to keep the peace. I thought peace meant love. I was wrong.

I started feeling like I had to earn your attention. Like affection was something I had to deserve instead of something we shared naturally.

There were nights I held you and felt absolutely nothing change inside you. That disconnect scared me more than distance ever could.

I hated how easily you could pull away emotionally while I stayed fully attached. That imbalance did something ugly to my self-worth.

I wanted you badly sometimes. In that raw, physical way where words don't help. I wanted to kiss you until everything slowed down and the doubts shut up for a moment.

I don't think you understood how much effort it took for me to not sound desperate when all I wanted was for you to stay close.

I started questioning my own value. Wondering if I was enough, or if loving me just became inconvenient for you.

I missed you even when you were right beside me.

That kind of loneliness messes with your head.

There were moments I pulled away emotionally just to see if you'd notice. You didn't. That hurt more than I expected.

I hated how jealous thoughts crept in even when I didn't want them to. Fear does that. It makes you imagine replacements before they even exist.

I still remember the weight of you against me when you relaxed. That closeness felt grounding. Losing it felt like losing stability.

I didn't want control. I wanted consistency. I wanted to know where I stood without having to guess every day.

I felt guilty for wanting more from you. As if asking for effort made me demanding.

I started shrinking my expectations so I wouldn't be disappointed. That's when I realized I was losing myself.

I loved you in ways that made me feel exposed. Unprotected. Like I gave you parts of me without keeping backups.

I don't think you ever saw how close I was to breaking while still trying to look calm for you.

I started feeling angry and didn't know where to put it. I couldn't throw it at you because I was scared, you'd leave. I couldn't throw it at myself because I was already exhausted. So, it just sat there, heavy, unresolved.

I hated how calm you looked while I was unravelling quietly. Like we were in two different relationships and only one of us noticed.

There were nights I kissed you harder than usual. Not out of passion alone — out of fear. Like if I could just feel you closer, maybe you wouldn't slip away.

I started feeling stupid for caring this much. For noticing small changes. For feeling hurt by things, you called "nothing."

I didn't want reassurance anymore. I wanted effort. I wanted proof that I wasn't the only one holding this together.

Sometimes I'd look at you and feel both love and resentment at the same time. That combination messes with your head more than hate ever could.

I stopped sharing my insecurities with you. Not because they disappeared — because I didn't feel safe putting them in your hands anymore.

I missed the way we used to touch without tension. When closeness didn't come with questions attached to it.

I felt like I was constantly waiting for you to choose me again. That waiting drained something important out of me.

I hated how often I questioned myself instead of questioning what was happening between us.

There were moments I wanted to pull you into me and just stay there. No talking. No fixing. Just holding on to something that felt real.

I noticed how easily you moved through days while I was stuck replaying conversations. That imbalance hurt deeply.

I felt replaceable in ways I didn't know how to explain without sounding insecure.

I started wondering if loving me had become too much work for you.

I hated how much power your mood had over me. One good moment could lift me. One cold one could destroy me.

I don't think you ever saw how much energy it took for me to keep showing up when I felt unwanted.

There were times I wanted to walk away just to see if you'd stop me. I didn't. I was scared of what silence would say.

I missed feeling chosen without having to ask for it.

I don't think you meant to hurt me. That almost makes it worse.

I stayed longer than I should have because I kept hoping you'd return to who you were with me at the beginning.

wait—something hitting my mind

Sometimes I catch myself thinking about things that never happened but feel so real that my chest tightens anyway. Like us somewhere cold, snow everywhere, music playing softly in the background — that stupid Sia snowman song you'd probably tease me for liking — and you laughing while pulling me into the snow just to dance for no reason. No choreography, no audience, just us moving badly, slipping, holding each other so we don't fall. I always imagined your hands would be freezing and I'd pull you closer just to warm you up, pretending it's about the cold when it's really about not wanting to let go.

I think about the way I'd kiss you then. Not rushed. Not hungry. Just slow. The kind of kiss that happens when time feels paused. Forehead first. Nose touching. That half-smile before lips meets. The kind of kiss where you breathe each other in before anything else happens. I wanted so many of those with you — the kind that don't need an excuse.

In my head, there's always this trip. Switzerland. I don't even know why. Maybe because it feels unreal, like something soft people plan when they believe in futures. You'd wake up before me, obviously. I'd open my eyes and see you sitting there with coffee, holding the mug with both hands because it's hot, and you'd hand it to me like it's nothing.

That small act — you giving me the first sip — that's the kind of intimacy I wanted with you. Quiet. Everyday. Undramatic.

I imagine us back in bed after that, not sleeping, just lying there. Your legs tangled with mine. My arm around you, your head on my chest. No phones. No conversations that need fixing. Just breathing. I think people underestimate how healing it is to be held without expectations. I wanted to give you that. I wanted that with you.

There are stupid little things too. Sharing chocolate and pretending I don't notice you eating most of it. Making breakfast together and messing it up because we're talking more than cooking. You stealing food from my plate and acting innocent. Pillow fights that start as jokes and end with us laughing so hard we forget why we started. Those moments don't look special from outside, but they build something real inside you.

I think about movie nights where we don't even finish the movie. You half-asleep on my shoulder, me pretending to watch while counting how many times you shift closer. Or sitting somewhere watching the sunset, not saying much, just holding hands like it's the most natural thing in the world.

I wanted that calm with you. That "nothing needs to be proved" kind of love.

And yeah, I wanted you physically too. I won't lie about that. I wanted the way your body would melt into mine when you trusted me. The warmth. The closeness. The way desire feels softer when it's mixed with safety. Not rushed, not rough, just deep and intentional. I wanted you to feel wanted without feeling pressured. Desired without feeling owned.

Most of all, I wanted us in those in-between moments. The ones people don't post. The ones that don't look exciting but feel like home. Just you and me doing normal things and choosing each other without effort.

None of this happened. I know that.
But it doesn't mean it wasn't real to me.

Sometimes the most painful part of loving someone isn't what you lost — it's the life you imagined and never got to live.

Ahhh my imaginations…

I started feeling like I was begging without actually begging. Like my silence was doing the asking for me. That kind of desperation changes how you see yourself.

I hated how much of my day revolved around your energy. If you were distant, everything felt off. If you were warm, I felt alive again. That dependency scared me, but not enough to leave.

There were moments I wanted to ask you straight up if you were already halfway gone. I didn't ask because I wasn't ready to hear the truth.

I don’t think you noticed how I slowly stopped expecting things from you. That wasn’t maturity. That was resignation.

I caught myself imagining you choosing someone else and felt sick for even thinking that. But fear plants pictures in your head whether you want them or not.

I wanted to hold you and feel like I still mattered. Not to prove anything. Just to feel grounded again.

I hated how my mind started making worst-case scenarios out of nothing. Overthinking became my default setting.

There were days I felt like I was annoying you just by existing. That feeling eats at you quietly.

I stopped feeling secure and started feeling tolerated.

That shift hurts more than rejection.

I loved you, but I was also constantly bracing myself. That’s not how love is supposed to feel.

I started noticing how often I was the one reaching out. Initiating. Trying. That imbalance felt humiliating.

There were moments I wanted to disappear just to see if you'd miss me. That thought scared me when it first appeared.

I hated how attached I still felt even when things were clearly falling apart.

I don't think you ever understood how much strength it took for me to stay calm while everything inside me was screaming.

I missed the version of us where love didn't feel like something I had to constantly protect.

I felt like I was slowly losing access to you, piece by piece, and there was nothing I could do about it.

I started doubting my own reality. Wondering if I was imagining the distance or if it was really there.

I didn't want reassurance anymore. I wanted to stop feeling like I was chasing it.

I hated how much I still wanted you even when I was clearly hurting.

That's when I realized I wasn't just scared of losing you — I was scared of being alone with what loving you had done to me.

I started feeling like I was disappearing inside the relationship. Not in a dramatic way. Just slowly. Like parts of me stopped asking for space because they knew there wouldn't be room.

I hated how I'd replay your words in my head, trying to figure out what you really meant. That habit made me feel small and obsessive, and I didn't recognize myself anymore.

There were moments I wanted to hurt myself emotionally just to feel something different. I'd imagine worst endings because at least pain felt familiar.

I stopped trusting my instincts. Every time I felt something was off, I convinced myself I was overreacting. That self-gaslighting messed me up.

I loved you so much that I accepted crumbs and told myself it was a full meal. Admitting that now makes my chest feel tight.

I hated how desperate my thoughts became. How often I wondered what you were doing, who you were with, whether you were thinking about me at all.

There were nights I wanted to be inside your arms just to feel safe again. Not romantic. Not sexual. Just safe.

I noticed how easily you could detach while I kept sinking deeper. That imbalance made me feel stupid for caring this much.

I felt ashamed of how much power you had over my emotions. Like my happiness was no longer mine.

I stopped telling myself this would get better. That hope had started hurting more than helping.

There were moments I fantasized about disappearing from your life just to see if it would affect you. That thought scared me because it felt too honest.

I hated how my body still wanted you even when my mind knew this wasn't healthy anymore.

I started believing I was hard to love. That thought didn’t come from nowhere — it grew slowly while loving you.

I missed being myself without worrying how it would land with you.

I noticed how tired my heart felt. Not broken. Just worn out from hoping.

I stopped expecting affection. When it came, it felt surprising instead of natural.

I felt like I was living in a constant state of emotional alert. Always ready for the next shift, the next silence, the next disappointment.

I hated how much I still wanted to be chosen by you, even after everything.

I didn't feel loved anymore. I felt tolerated. That difference changed something permanently inside me.

That's when I realized loving you had slowly turned into something that was hurting me more than it was holding me.

I stopped reacting the way I used to. Things that once hurt deeply started landing dull. That scared me more than pain ever did.

I noticed I wasn't crying anymore. Not because I was okay — because I was empty.

There were moments I felt detached from myself, like I was watching my own life from the outside and wondering how I let it get here.

I didn't miss you constantly anymore. I missed you in waves. Sudden, heavy, unpredictable.

I hated how calm I started feeling about the idea of losing you. That calm felt wrong.

I stopped imagining fixing things. I started imagining surviving without you.

There were nights I didn’t want comfort. I wanted to disappear into sleep and not think about anything at all.

I realized I was emotionally preparing myself for an ending you hadn't officially said out loud.

I stopped checking for signs that you cared. I didn't want to be disappointed anymore.

I felt distant even when we talked. Like the connection was already fading while words were still happening.

I noticed how little effort it took for you to be okay without me. That realization hit quietly and stayed.

I stopped asking myself what went wrong. I was too tired to analyse anymore.

There were moments I felt angry for no clear reason.

That anger had nowhere to go.

I didn't want answers. I wanted peace. That shift surprised me.

I felt guilty for how numb I was becoming. Like I was betraying my own feelings.

I noticed how my thoughts slowed down. Overthinking gave way to resignation.

I wasn't scared of losing you anymore. I was scared of what loving you had done to me.

I stopped hoping you'd change. That hope had already exhausted me.

I felt myself pulling back emotionally, not to protect my pride, but to protect what was left of me.

That's when I knew something inside me was shutting down quietly, without asking for permission.

I started feeling like something inside me was watching everything happen instead of feeling it. Like I'd already accepted the loss before it actually arrived.

There were moments I imagined you gone and felt… nothing. That scared me more than missing you ever did.

I caught myself smiling in situations where I should've felt sad. It felt wrong, like my emotions were misfiring.

I stopped telling people I was okay. I also stopped telling them I wasn't. Explaining felt pointless.

I noticed how easily I could think about you without emotion now. That numbness didn't feel like healing. It felt like damage.

There were nights I felt too tired to even miss you. I'd just lie there, empty, staring at nothing, waiting for sleep to take me out of my head.

I didn’t feel the urge to reach out anymore. Not because I was strong — because I was done hoping.

I felt disconnected from the version of me that loved you so intensely. Like that person had burned out and left me behind.

I noticed how calm I became around the idea of never hearing from you again. That calm felt unnatural.

There were moments I wondered if loving you had permanently changed how I experience attachment.

I stopped replaying memories. Not because they stopped hurting — because they stopped feeling important.

I felt like I was carrying emotional scars no one could see or understand. That invisibility made it worse.

I didn't miss you the way people romanticize missing someone. I missed you like an absence that had already settled in.

I realized I wasn't angry at you anymore. I was angry at myself for letting it go this far.

I noticed how little space you took in my thoughts now compared to before. That shift felt like losing something twice.

There were days I questioned whether I'd ever feel that deeply again — and nights where I hoped I wouldn't.

I felt detached from intimacy itself. Like closeness now came with too many memories attached.

I stopped imagining conversations with you. That silence felt final.

I realized I wasn't waiting for you anymore. I was waiting for myself to feel normal again.

That's when I understood something had broken quietly inside me — not loudly enough for anyone to notice.

I don't miss you the way people talk about missing someone. I miss you like a habit that hasn't realized it's unnecessary yet.

There are moments I forget your voice and panic immediately, like my mind is erasing something it wasn't ready to let go of.

I catch myself wondering if you ever think about me when things are quiet. That thought shows up uninvited and leaves slowly.

I don't fantasize about fixing us anymore. I fantasize about not feeling like this.

Sometimes I imagine you reading these words and feeling nothing. That possibility hurts more than you leaving ever did.

I feel changed in ways I don't know how to explain to anyone else. Like loving you rewired parts of me permanently.

There are days I feel normal and then suddenly remember how deeply I loved you, and it feels like discovering a scar I forgot existed.

I don’t crave closeness the same way anymore. Desire now comes with hesitation, like my body remembers consequences my mind hasn’t caught up to.

I feel detached from the idea of “forever” now. Promises sound heavier than they should.

I don't hate you. I hate how much of myself I lost trying to keep you.

There are moments I feel like I imagined our intensity. Like maybe I felt everything alone and called it love.

I don’t know how to explain the emptiness that followed you. It’s not loud. It’s not dramatic. It’s just… there.

I stopped romanticizing pain. Now it just feels like evidence of how deeply I once cared.

I notice how guarded I am now. How slow I am to trust. Loving you taught me caution the hard way.

Sometimes I wish I could feel everything again, even the hurt, just to know I'm still capable of that depth.

I don't think I'll ever forget you. Not because you were perfect — but because you mattered at the wrong time.

I feel like a quieter version of myself now. Not weaker. Just less willing to bleed openly.

I don't wait for you anymore. That doesn't feel like victory. It feels like acceptance settling in.

If I'm honest, loving you changed me in ways I'll never fully undo. And maybe that's okay.

This is me choosing to live with what happened instead of letting it define me.

Not healed.
Just still here.

FOR HER

I don't know if you'll ever read this, but this is the last time I'm talking to you like this. Not because I ran out of things to say — I could bleed words forever — but because I'm done leaving pieces of myself at your door hoping you'll notice.

I loved you in ways I never loved anyone. I didn't protect myself from you. I didn't keep backups. I didn't keep pride. I didn't keep exits. I stood there fully exposed and still chose you every time you doubted me. That's not weakness. That's devotion without safety gear.

You never had to touch me to own me. You already lived in my head, my sleep, my reactions, my silence. I would've sat there my whole life just listening to your talk, just letting you say whatever you wanted to me, even if it hurt, even if it broke me — because hearing your voice was enough. I didn't need your body. I needed your presence. And even that became too much to ask for.

I let you hurt me in ways I didn't even know how to explain to myself. I let you question my intentions. I let you doubt my loyalty. I let you make me feel like loving you was something I had to defend.

I accepted being misunderstood because losing you felt worse than losing myself.

There are things you'll never know. How many times I stayed quiet just to keep your calm. How many times I swallowed words that would've protected me. How many nights I broke down alone and still showed up for you the next day like nothing happened. I didn't do those things to look good. I did them because I loved you in a way that didn't know how to stop.

And the worst part is — I would've kept doing it. I would've kept shrinking. I would've kept bleeding silently. I would've stayed in that pain if it meant staying connected to you. That's the part that scares me now. Not that you left — but that I would've destroyed myself completely if you hadn't.

This book isn't revenge. It's evidence. Evidence that I was real. That I didn't imagine it. That I didn't exaggerate. That I didn't pretend. I loved you honestly, obsessively, destructively — and still never tried to control you. I just wanted to be chosen without begging.

I'm letting you go now. Not cleanly. Not bravely. Just finally.

And if you ever wonder whether someone could've loved you more gently and more fiercely at the same time — this, is it. This was me. And this is the last time I'm leaving my heart open on a page for you.

FOR SWEET FELLOWS

You think I'm a bad guy.
That's okay. It's easier that way.

You didn't see what happened when no one was watching. You didn't see the nights I stayed up just to listen. You didn't see me choosing silence over self-respect because I didn't want to hurt her. You didn't see me saying "it's fine" when it wasn't, just so she wouldn't feel pressured.

I never touched her when she didn't want to be touched. I never forced closeness. I never demanded affection. I asked for conversation. For honesty. For presence. That's it. I would've lived my whole life without her body if it meant I could just talk to her, hear her, understand her. I didn't need anything physical. I needed connection.

You saw the aftermath and decided who I was. You didn't see the effort. You didn't see the patience. You didn't see how much of myself I erased just to make her feel safe. You didn't see me take blame for things I didn't do just to keep the peace.

I'm not perfect. I got emotional. I got scared. I loved deeply. If that makes me a bad person in your story, then fine. Carry that version of me. Just know it's incomplete.

I know what I gave.
I know how I stayed.
And I know I didn't hurt her on purpose.

That has to be enough — even if you never believe it.

I loved the way I knew how.
I stayed as long as I could.

And now I'm letting this rest.

Nothing more to explain.
Nothing left to prove.

This is where I stop talking
and start living again.

ABOUT THE AUTHOR

Vivek Maurya writes the way silence would, if it ever got tired of being quiet.

He won't call himself a writer, just someone who felt too much and chose words instead of running.

His writing isn't here to heal you or teach you anything. It just sits beside you when things feel heavy.

I adore you until it hurts is his way of saying what stayed unsaid for too long.

He's probably still overthinking somewhere on
Instagram: @penmanviv

THANK YOU TO THE READERS

If you made it this far,
thank you for staying.

Thank you for reading gently.
Thank you for feeling without rushing.
Thank you for not judging the pain.

I hope you found a piece of yourself here,
or at least felt a little less alone.

Take care of your heart.
And close this book slowly.

Goodbye.